## Program Authors

Peter Afflerbach

Camille Blachowicz

Candy Dawson Boyd

Elena Izquierdo

Connie Juel

Edward Kame'enui

Donald Leu

Jeanne R. Paratore

P. David Pearson

Sam Sebesta

Deborah Simmons

Alfred Tatum

Sharon Vaughn

Susan Watts Taffe

Karen Kring Wixson

Glenview, Illinois • Boston, Massachusetts • Chandler, Arizona • Upper Saddle River, New Jersey

*We dedicate Reading Street to*
*Peter Jovanovich.*

*His wisdom, courage,*
*and passion for education*
*are an inspiration to us all.*

**About the Cover Artist**
Rob Hefferan likes to reminisce about the simple life he had as a child growing up in Cheshire, when his biggest worry was whether to have fish fingers or Alphabetti Spaghetti for tea. The faces, colors, and shapes from that time are a present-day inspiration for his artwork.

ISBN-13: 978-0-328-48106-4
ISBN-10:    0-328-48106-8
6 7 8 9 10 V011 14 13 12 11

Dear Reader,

What do you think of Reading Street so far? You've learned lots of letters and sounds and words. Have AlphaBuddy and your *My Skills Buddy* helped you along the way?

On the next part of our trip, you will read about plants and animals, and there will be a special visit to a very large beanstalk.

So hop on board, and let's get going. There's lots more to learn.

Sincerely,
The Authors

# Look at Us!

**How are animals and plants unique?**

**Week 2**

NATURE SPY

Big Book

Nonfiction • Science

**Nature Spy** by Shelley Rotner

# Unit 2 Contents

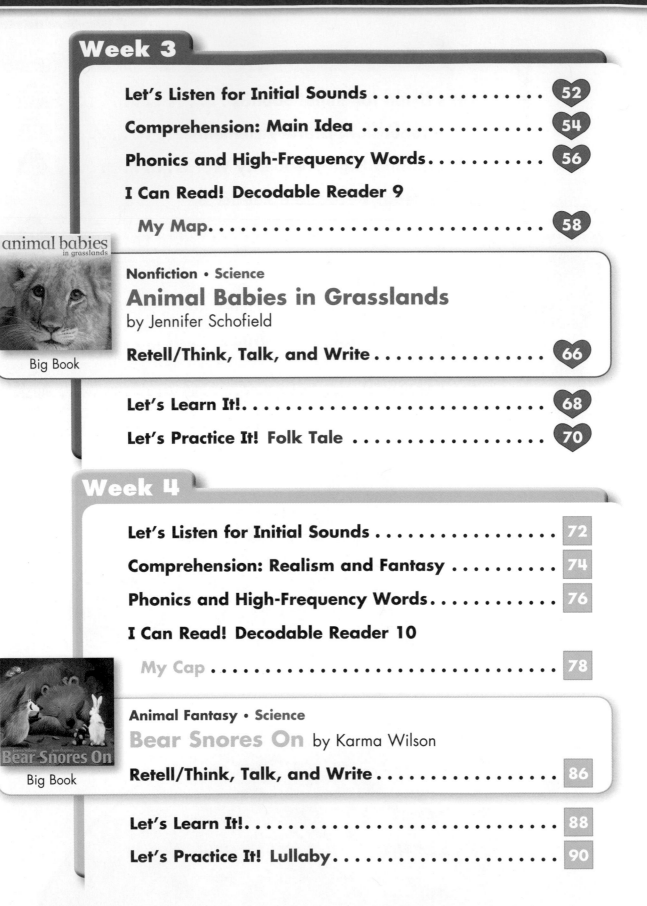

Don Leu
**The Internet Guy**

Right before our eyes, the nature of reading and learning is changing. The Internet and other technologies create new opportunities, new solutions, and new literacies. New reading comprehension skills are required online. They are increasingly important to our students and our society.

Those of us on the Reading Street team are here to help you on this new, and very exciting, journey.

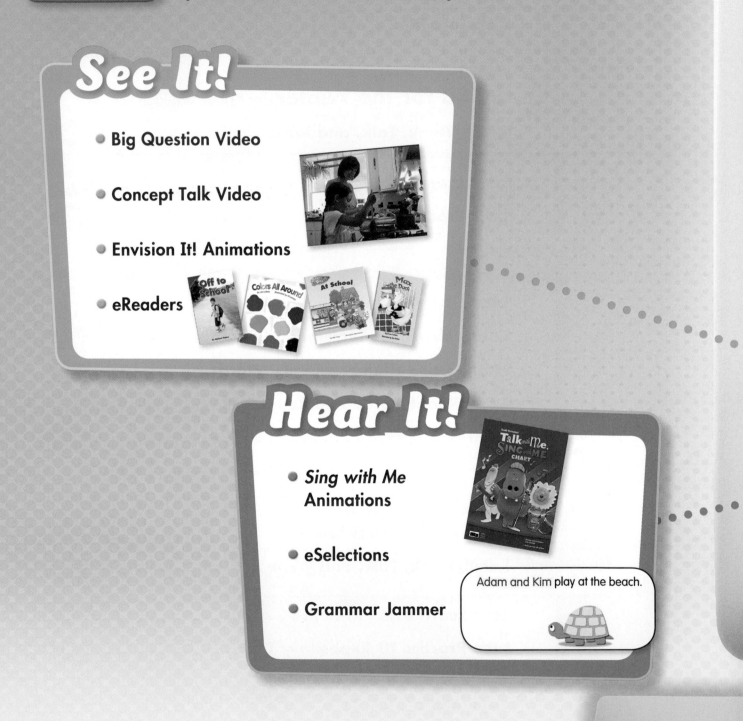

## See It!

- Big Question Video
- Concept Talk Video
- Envision It! Animations
- eReaders

## Hear It!

- *Sing with Me* Animations
- eSelections
- Grammar Jammer

Adam and Kim play at the beach.

Concept Talk Video

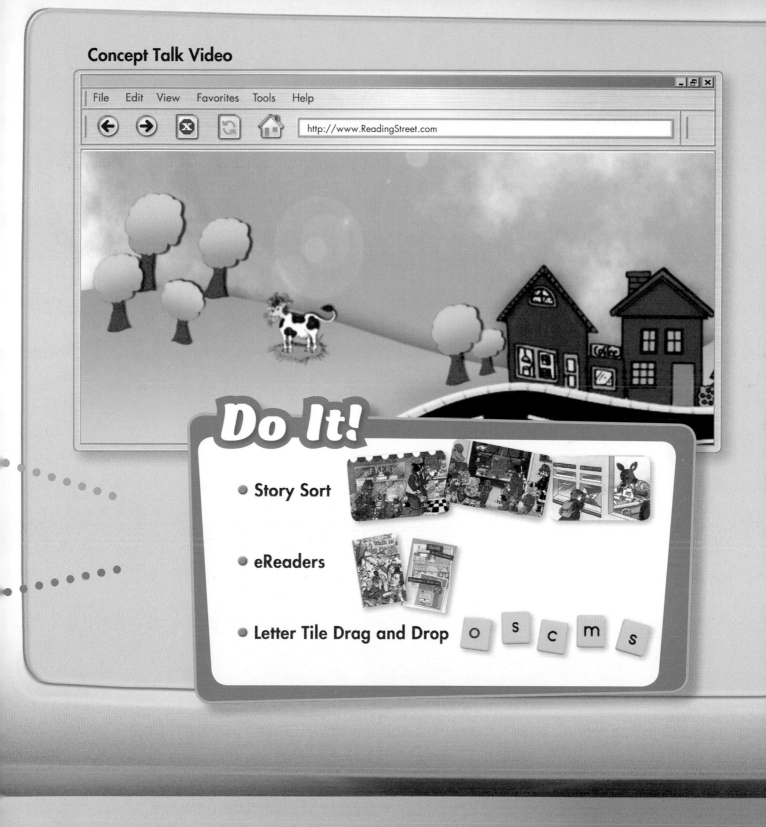

| File | Edit | View | Favorites | Tools | Help |

http://www.ReadingStreet.com

## Do It!

- Story Sort

- eReaders

- Letter Tile Drag and Drop   o   s   c   m   s

# Look at Us!

**THE BIG**

**How are animals and plants unique?**

# Let's Listen for

## Initial Sounds

*Read Together*

● Say *Ann, Al, Andy.* What sound do you hear at the beginning of these names?

■ Find three things that begin with /a/, like *Ann.*

▲ Point to these pictures and say these words: *bed, pillow, rug.* Do they begin with the same sound? What about *ant, alligator, astronaut?*

★ What rhymes with *Ann?*

**READING STREET ONLINE**
**BIG QUESTION VIDEO**
www.ReadingStreet.com

12

abcde
fghij
klmn
opqr
stuv
wxyz

**Objectives**
● Tell how facts, ideas, characters, settings, or events are the same and/or different.

**Comprehension**

# Envision It!

## Compare and Contrast

**READING STREET ONLINE**
**ENVISION IT! ANIMATIONS**
www.ReadingStreet.com

Objectives
- Use what you know about letters and their sounds to read words in a list and in sentences or stories.
- Know and read at least 25 often-used words.

Phonics

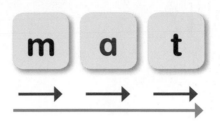

# Short Aa

## Words I Can Blend

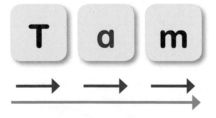

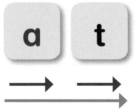

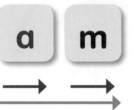

## Words I Can Read

have

is

## Sentences I Can Read

**1.** I have a mat.

**2.** The mat is little.

**3.** Tam is little.

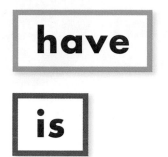

**Objectives**
● Point out the common sounds that letters stand for. ● Use what you know about letters and their sounds to read words in a list and in sentences or stories. ● Know and read at least 25 often-used words.

**Phonics**

# I Can Read!

## Decodable Reader

● Short *a*
am
Tam
mat
at

■ High-Frequency Words
I
am
is
little
have
a
the

▲ Read the story.

Decodable Reader 7

# A Little Mat

Written by Alex Altman
Illustrated by Mary Stern

I am Tam.

Is Tam little?

Tam is little.

I have a mat.

Is the mat little?

The mat is little.

Tam is at the mat.

# Envision It! | Retell

**Flowers**
by Vijaya Khisty Bodach
Gail Saunders-Smith, PhD, Consulting Editor

**Big Book**

# Think, Talk, and Write

1. Tell about a unique flower you have seen. **Text to Self**

2. How are a rose and a cauliflower alike? How are they different?

**Compare and Contrast**

3. Look back and write.

# Let's Learn It!

## Vocabulary

- ● What do you see that is yellow?
- ■ What do you see that is purple?
- ▲ What do you see that is orange?

## Listening and Speaking

- ● What happens first in the story?
- ■ What happens next in the story?
- ▲ What happens last in the story?

**Vocabulary**

# Color Words

yellow

purple

orange

# Listen for Sequence

Be a good listener!

# Let's Practice It!

## Fable

● Listen to the fable.

■ How are the two characters different?

▲ What is the field like in summer? in winter?

★ How is this story like "The Boy Who Cried 'Wolf!'"?

♥ What new expression does this fable teach you?

# The Ant and the Grasshopper

**1**

# Let's Listen for

## Initial Sounds

**Read Together**

● Say *Sam, Seth, Sue.* What sound do you hear at the beginning of these names?

■ Point to the sun. Find three things that begin with /s/, like *sun.*

▲ Point to these pictures and say the words: *table, soap, fork.* Do they begin the same? What about *salt, socks, silverware?*

★ Which words rhyme? socks/clocks? Sam/Sally? Sue/you?

♥ What sounds might you hear in a school lunchroom?

**READING STREET ONLINE**
**BIG QUESTION VIDEO**
www.ReadingStreet.com

32

33

**Objectives**

● Point out parts of a story including where it takes place, the characters, and the main events.

## Envision It!

### Literary Elements

**READING STREET ONLINE**
**ENVISION IT! ANIMATIONS**
www.ReadingStreet.com

## Characters

## Setting

34

## Plot

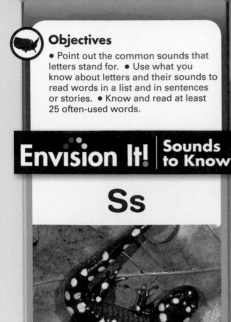
Phonics

# 🎯 Initial *Ss*

## Words I Can Blend

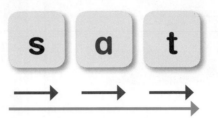

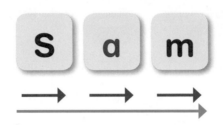

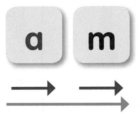

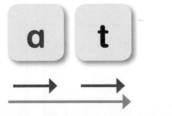

## Words I Can Read

have

is

## Sentences I Can Read

**1.** I have Sam.

**2.** Sam is little.

**3.** Sam is a 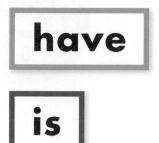.

**Objectives**
● Point out the common sounds that letters stand for. ● Use what you know about letters and their sounds to read words in a list and in sentences or stories. ● Know and read at least 25 often-used words.

**Phonics**

# I Can Read!

### Decodable Reader

● Consonant *Ss*
  Sam
  sat

■ High-Frequency Words
  I
  am
  have
  a
  the
  is

▲ Read the story.

**READING STREET ONLINE**
**DECODABLE eREADERS**
**www.ReadingStreet.com**

**Decodable Reader 8**

# Sam and Tam

Written by Paul Thomas
Illustrated by Katie Snell

I am Sam.

I have a mat.

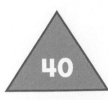

Sam sat at the mat.

I am Tam.

Tam is at the mat.

Tam sat at the mat.

Tam sat.
Sam sat.

# Envision It! | Retell

**Big Book**

NATURE SPY
written by SHELLEY ROTNER and KEN KREISLER
photographs by SHELLEY ROTNER

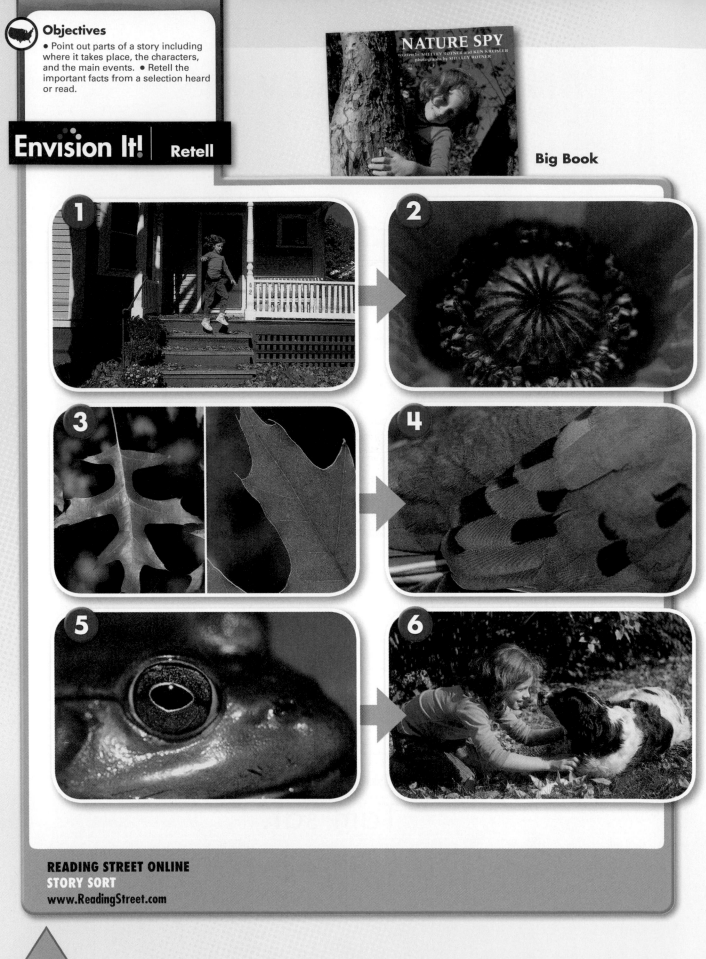

# Think, Talk, and Write

**1.** What did you learn about nature from the story?

Text to Self

**2.** Where does *Nature Spy* take place?

🎯 Setting

**3.** Look back and write.

# Let's Learn It!

## Vocabulary

- ● Talk about the pictures.
- ■ What grows near your home?

## Listening and Speaking

- ● Follow AlphaBuddy's directions.
- ■ Act like an animal.

Vocabulary

# Nature Words

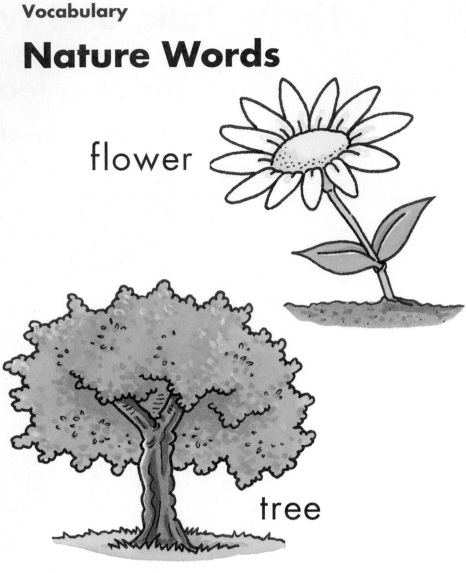

flower

tree

leaf

grass

**48**

# Listen for Directions

Be a good listener!

49

# Let's Practice It!

## Fairy Tale

● Listen to the fairy tale.

■ How can you tell this is a fairy tale?

▲ Why does the elf grant Josef three wishes?

★ How do Josef and Anna waste two wishes?

♥ Tell why you think people like to read and listen to fairy tales.

# The Three Wishes

**Objectives**
● Point out the syllables, or parts, in words you say. ● Point out groups of spoken words that begin with the same sound. ● Say the sound at the beginning of spoken one-syllable words.

# Let's Listen for

## Initial Sounds

Read Together

● Say *Pat, Pam, Pete.* What sound do you hear at the beginning of these names?

■ Find three things in the picture that begin like *Pat.*

▲ Point to these pictures and say the words: *paper, panda, penguin.* Do they begin the same? What about *pig, door, street?*

★ Name a color you see in the picture. Clap the word parts. How many claps?

**READING STREET ONLINE**
**BIG QUESTION VIDEO**
www.ReadingStreet.com

53

**Objectives**
- Use the words and/or the pictures to tell what an article is about, and tell some details.

**Comprehension**

# Envision It!

## Main Idea

**READING STREET ONLINE**
**ENVISION IT! ANIMATIONS**
www.ReadingStreet.com

School

**Phonics**

# Initial and Final *Pp*

## Words I Can Blend

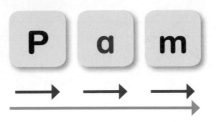

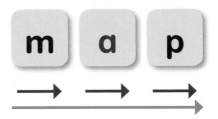

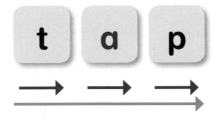

## Words I Can Read

| we |
|----|

| my |
|----|

| like |
|----|

## Sentences I Can Read

**1.** We have a map.

**2.** We like the map.

**3.** My map is little.

**Objectives**
● Point out the common sounds that letters stand for. ● Use what you know about letters and their sounds to read words in a list and in sentences or stories. ● Know and read at least 25 often-used words.

**Phonics**

# I Can Read!

## Decodable Reader

● Consonant *Pp*
Pam
map
tap
pat

■ High-Frequency Words

| | |
|---|---|
| I | am |
| have | a |
| the | my |
| we | like |

▲ Read the story.

Decodable Reader 9

# My Map

Written by Jerry Moore
Illustrated by Chris Brown

I am Pam.

I have a map.

The map sat at the mat.

I tap my map.

We tap the map.

We pat at the map.

We like the map.

# Envision It! | Retell

animal babies
in grasslands

**Big Book**

1
2
3
4
5
6

# Think, Talk, and Write

**1.** How are most animal babies the same? Text to World

**2.** What is *Animal Babies in Grasslands* about?

Main Idea

**3.** Look back and write.

**Objectives**

• Listen closely to speakers by facing them and asking questions to help you better understand the information.
• Follow rules for discussions, including taking turns and speaking one at a time.

# Let's Learn It!

## Vocabulary

● Talk about the pictures.

■ Where do these animal babies live?

## Listening and Speaking

● Say one thing about yourself.

■ Listen to others talk about themselves.

▲ Retell facts about a friend.

Vocabulary

# Words for Animal Babies

puppy

kitten

chick

calf

# Discussion

Be a good speaker!

**Objectives**
- Ask and answer questions about texts read aloud. • Discuss the big idea, or *theme*, of a folk tale or fable and connect it to your own life.
- Point out the phrases and characters that appear in many different stories from around the world.

# Let's Practice It!

## Folk Tale

● Listen to the folk tale.

■ Where and when does the story take place?

▲ Why does Anansi put his hat back on?

★ Tell about Anansi. What is he like?

♥ Share ideas about what you learn from Anansi that can help you.

✱ What questions do you have about this folk tale?

# Anansi's Hat Shaking Dance

70

**Objectives**
• Point out the syllables, or parts, in words you say. • Point out groups of spoken words that begin with the same sound. • Say the sound at the beginning of spoken one-syllable words.

# Let's Listen for

*Read Together*

## Initial Sounds

● Say *Carl, Cam, Cate.* What sound do you hear at the beginning of these names?

■ Point to the cart in the picture. Find three things that begin with /k/, like *cart.*

▲ Name other words that begin with /k/.

★ Point to and say, *Carrots and cucumbers are in the cart.* What sound do you hear repeated?

♥ Say *cucumber.* Clap the word parts. How many claps?

**READING STREET ONLINE**
**BIG QUESTION VIDEO**
www.ReadingStreet.com

72

**Comprehension**

# Envision It!

## Realism and Fantasy

**READING STREET ONLINE**
**ENVISION IT! ANIMATIONS**
www.ReadingStreet.com

**Objectives**
- Notice that new words are made when letters are changed, added, or taken away.
- Know and read at least 25 often-used words.
- Use what you know about letters and their sounds to read words in a list and in sentences or stories.

**Envision It!** | **Sounds to Know**

## Cc

### cactus

**READING STREET ONLINE**
**ALPHABET CARDS**
www.ReadingStreet.com

**Phonics**

# Initial and Final *Cc*

## Words I Can Blend

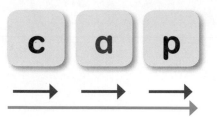

c a p

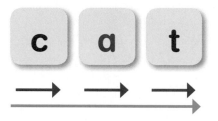

c a t

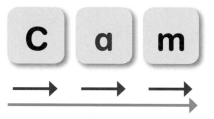

C a m

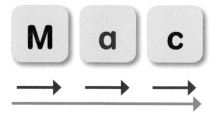

M a c

## Words I Can Read

we

my

like

## Sentences I Can Read

**1.** I like Cam.

**2.** We like to sit.

**3.** We like my cat.

# I Can Read!

## Decodable Reader

● Consonant Cc
Cam
Mac
cap

■ High-Frequency Words

| | |
|---|---|
| I | am |
| we | have |
| a | is |
| the | my |
| like | |

▲ Read the story.

**READING STREET ONLINE**
**DECODABLE eREADERS**
www.ReadingStreet.com

# My Cap
Written by Sue Bear
Illustrated by Lori Burk

**Decodable Reader 10**

I am Cam.
I am Mac.

We have a cap.

Cam is at the cap.

Is the cap my cap?

Mac is at the cap.

Is the cap my cap?

I like my cap.

# Envision It! | Retell

**Bear Snores On** **Big Book**

karma wilson   jane chapman

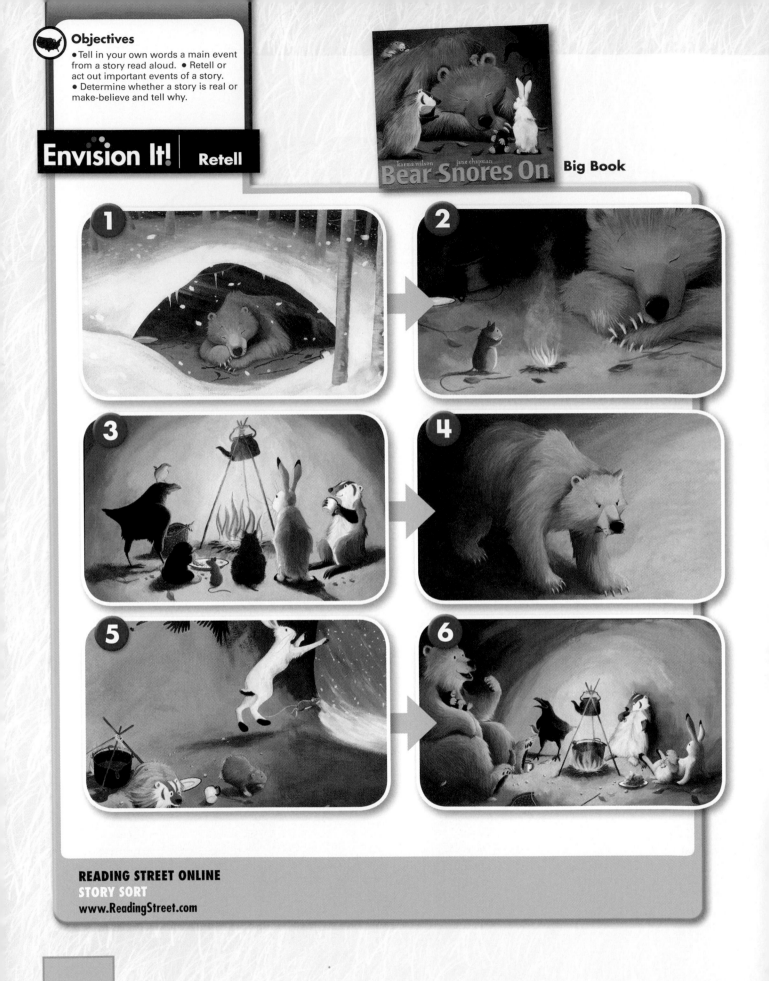

# Think, Talk, and Write

**1.** What does a bear do in the winter? Text to World

**2.** Which story is about real animals? Which is about make-believe animals?

Realism and Fantasy

**3.** Look back and write.

**Objectives**
• Listen closely to speakers by facing them and asking questions to help you better understand the information.
• Follow rules for discussions, including taking turns and speaking one at a time.

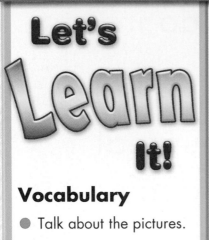

## Let's Learn It!

### Vocabulary

● Talk about the pictures.

■ Which season is your favorite?

### Listening and Speaking

● Where do AlphaBuddy's stories take place?

### Vocabulary

# Words for Nature

spring

summer

fall

winter

# Listen for Setting

Be a good listener!

# Let's Practice It!

## Lullaby

● Listen to the lullaby.

■ Sing the lullaby. Sway in time to its rhythm.

▲ Which words in the lullaby rhyme?

★ Who is often a main character in a lullaby? Why?

♥ Which part of the lullaby is make-believe?

# Rock-a-Bye, Baby

**1**

# Let's Listen for

## Initial Sounds

*Read Together*

● Say *Isabel, Izzy, Inga.* What sound do you hear at the beginning of these names?

■ Find three things that begin with /i/, like *Isabel.*

▲ Point to these pictures: *ink, iguana, igloo.* Do they begin the same? What about *insects, books, posters?*

★ Say *inventor.* Clap the word parts. How many claps?

♥ What sounds would you hear in a library? What kind of voice should you use?

# Envision It!

## Sequence

READING STREET ONLINE
ENVISION IT! ANIMATIONS
www.ReadingStreet.com

## Envision It! | Sounds to Know

**Ii**

**Igloo**

READING STREET ONLINE
ALPHABET CARDS
www.ReadingStreet.com

Phonics

## Short *Ii*

## Words I Can Blend

s i t

T i m

t i p

p i t

s i p

## Words I Can Read

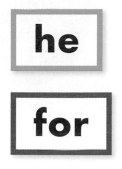

he

for

## Sentences I Can Read

1. He is a cat.

2. The cat is for Tim.

3. He can sit for Tim.

**Objectives**
● Point out the common sounds that letters stand for. ● Use what you know about letters and their sounds to read words in a list and in sentences or stories. ● Know and read at least 25 often-used words.

**Phonics**

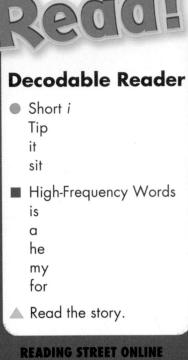

# I Can Read!

## Decodable Reader

● Short *i*
Tip
it
sit

■ High-Frequency Words
is
a
he
my
for

▲ Read the story.

**READING STREET ONLINE**
**DECODABLE eREADERS**
www.ReadingStreet.com

# Tip and Pat

Written by Kate Brand
Illustrated by Carl Johnson

**Decodable Reader 11**

Tip is a cat.

He is my cat.

Pat is a cat.

He is my cat.

It is for Tip.

It is for Pat.

Sit, Tip, sit.
Sit, Pat, sit.

**Objectives**
• Retell the important facts from a selection heard or read.
• Connect what you read to your own experiences, to other things you have read or heard, and to the world around you. • Describe the events of a story in order.

# Envision It! | Retell

A bed for the winter

**Big Book**

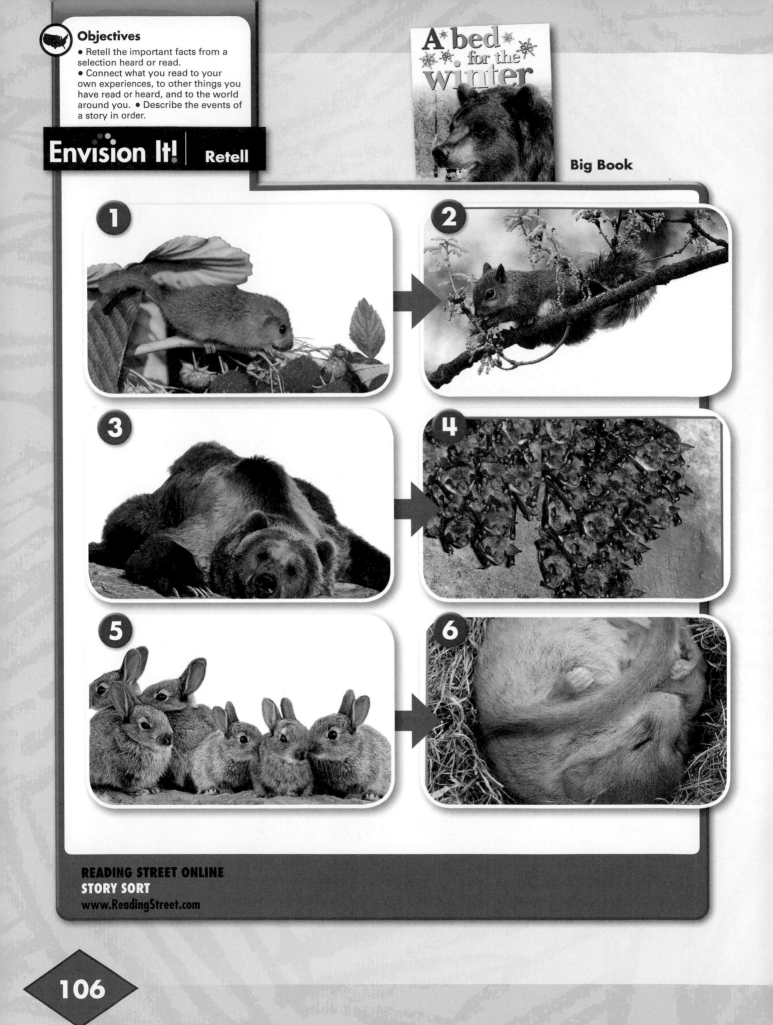

# Think, Talk, and Write

**1.** Which bed reminded you of *Bear Snores On*? Text to Text

**2.** Where does the dormouse go first in the story? Where does she go last?

 Sequence

**3.** Look back and write.

**Objectives**
● Understand and use new words that name actions, directions, positions, the order of something, and places.
● Share information and ideas by speaking clearly and using proper language.

# Let's Learn It!

## Vocabulary

● Talk about the pictures.

■ What do you do to get ready for school? Use sequence words.

## Listening and Speaking

● What do the clocks look like?

■ What do the dogs look like?

Vocabulary

# Sequence Words

first

second

next

last

# Give a Description

Be a good speaker!

## Let's Practice It!

### Nursery Rhyme

● Listen to the rhyme.

■ Recite the rhyme. Clap your hands to show the beats.

▲ How does Jack feel about his house? How can you tell?

★ Tell about a time when it rained on you. Did you feel like these animals felt?

**Objectives**
● Say the sound at the beginning of spoken one-syllable words.

# Let's Listen for

## Initial Sounds

*Read Together*

● Say the sound you hear at the beginning of *in, ask, sign, pears, cast*.

■ Point to the picture of *in*. Find a picture that begins with /i/, with /a/, with /s/, with /p/, with /k/.

▲ Name other words that begin with /i/, /a/, /s/, /p/, /k/.

**READING STREET ONLINE**
**BIG QUESTION VIDEO**
www.ReadingStreet.com

113

**Objectives**
● Determine whether a story is real or make-believe and tell why.

Comprehension

# Envision It!

## Realism and Fantasy

**READING STREET ONLINE**
**ENVISION IT! ANIMATIONS**
www.ReadingStreet.com

114

Envision It! | Sounds to Know

**Ii**

**igloo**

READING STREET ONLINE
ALPHABET CARDS
www.ReadingStreet.com

Phonics

# Short *Ii*

## Words I Can Blend

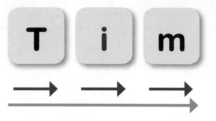

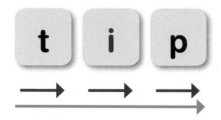

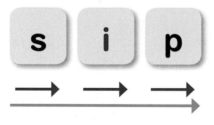

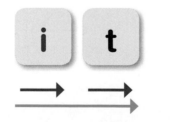

## Words I Can Read

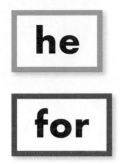

he

for

## Sentences I Can Read

**1.** He is my cat, Pip.

**2.** Pip can sit for Tim.

**3.** He can tap it.

**Objectives**
• Point out the common sounds that letters stand for. • Use what you know about letters and their sounds to read words in a list and in sentences or stories. • Know and read at least 25 often-used words.

**Phonics**

# I Can Read!

## Decodable Reader

● Short *i*
sit
Tim
tip
it

■ High-Frequency Words

| | |
|---|---|
| I | am |
| have | he |
| is | my |
| we | a |
| for | |

▲ Read the story.

**READING STREET ONLINE**
**DECODABLE eREADERS**
www.ReadingStreet.com

**Decodable Reader 12**

# Tim and Sam

Written by Joei Shavitz
Illustrated by Lawrence Paul

I am Sam.
I sit.

119

Tim sat.
I have Tim.

He is my cat.

I pat Tim.

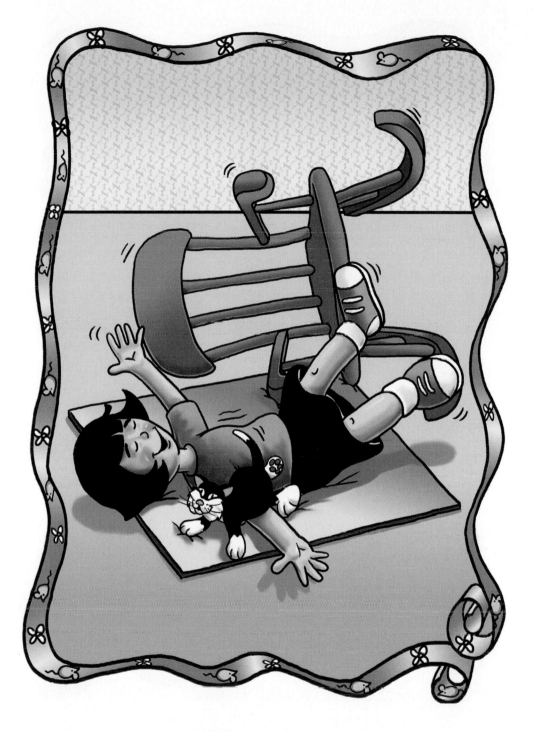

We tip.

I am Sam.
I sit.

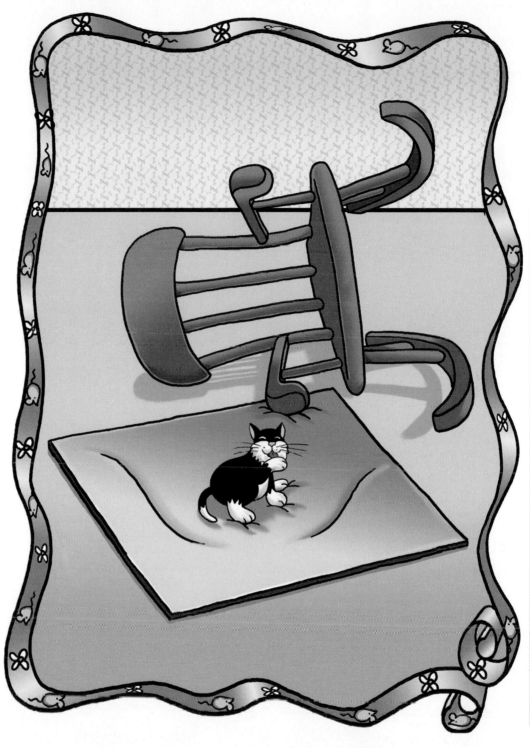

It is a mat for Tim.

**Objectives**
● Tell in your own words a main event from a story read aloud. ● Retell or act out important events of a story.
● Connect what you read to other things you have read or heard.
● Determine whether a story is real or make-believe and tell why.

**Jack and the Beanstalk**
from You Read to Me, I'll Read to You
by Mary Ann Hoberman
Illustrated by Natalia Vasquez

**Big Book**

# Envision It! | Retell

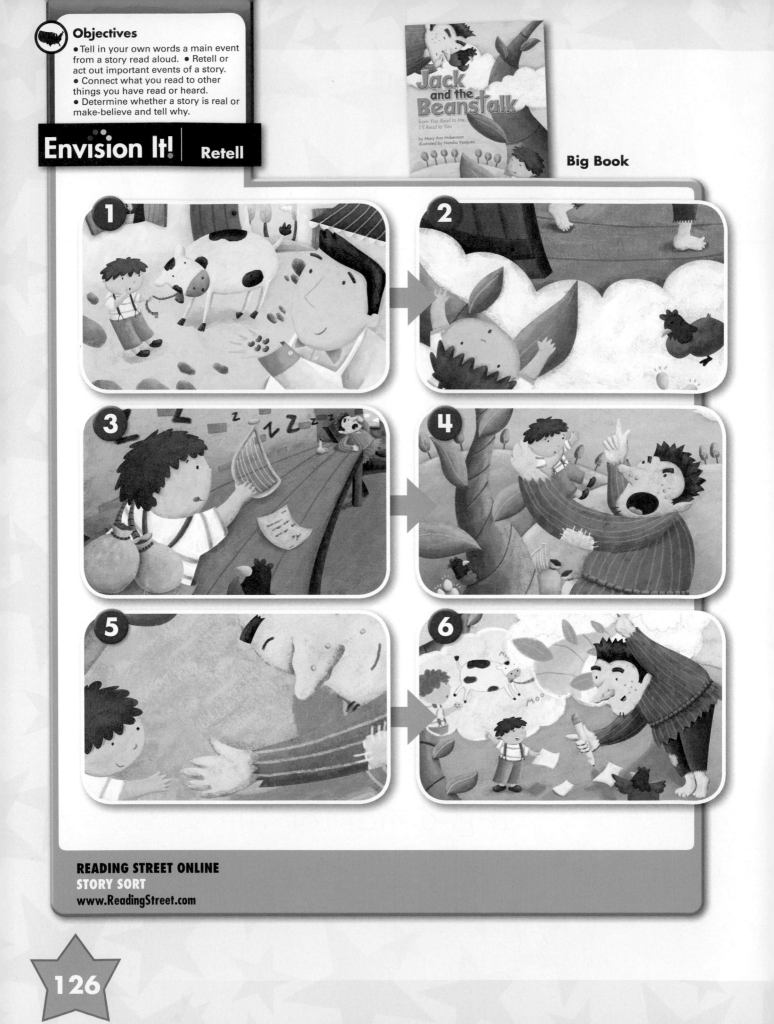

# Think, Talk, and Write

**1.** How are the plants in *Flowers* and *Jack and the Beanstalk* the same? How are they different? **Text to Text**

**2.** Which story is real?

Which is make-believe?

Realism and Fantasy

**3.** Look back and write.

# Let's Learn It!

## Vocabulary

● Talk about the picture.

■ Raise your right hand.

▲ Raise your left hand.

## Listening and Speaking

● What happens in the story?

Vocabulary

# Direction Words

left          right

# Listen for Plot

Be a good listener!

# Let's Practice It!

## Expository Text

● Look at the title and the pictures. What will the selection be about?

■ Listen to the selection.

▲ How do roots help a plant?

★ Where are the leaves on a plant?

♥ What does the author tell about first? second? third? last?

# Parts of a Plant

Leaf

Roots

130

Flower

Stem

# Words for Things That Go

airplane

bike

truck

car

bus

van

boat

train

# Words for Colors

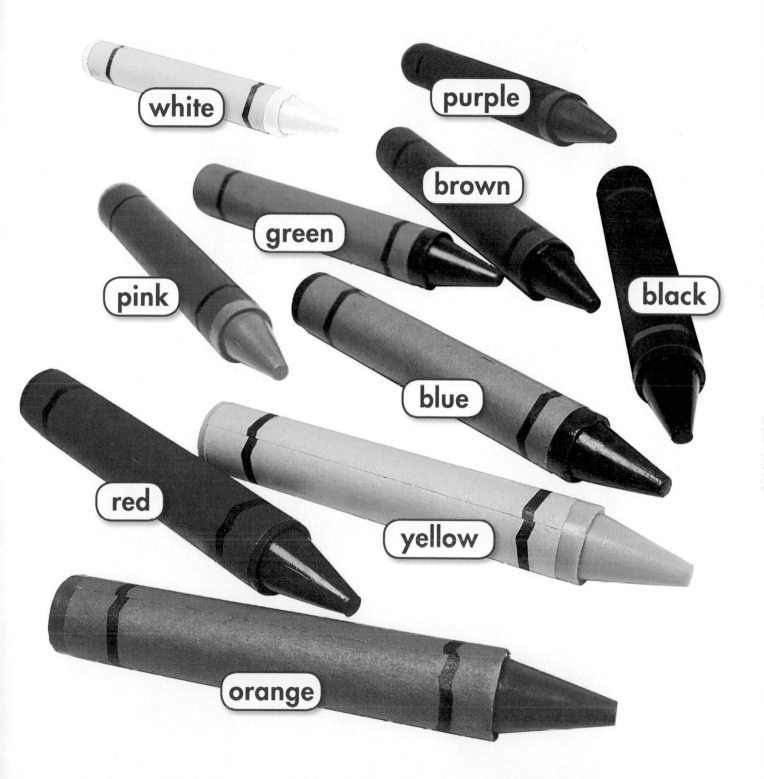

white

purple

brown

green

pink

black

blue

red

yellow

orange

# Words for Shapes

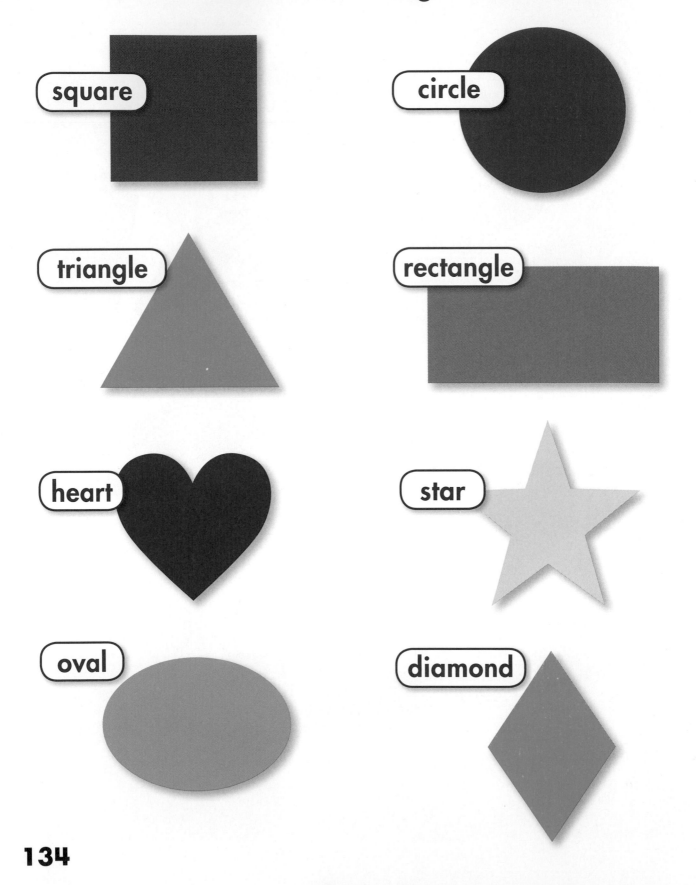

square

circle

triangle

rectangle

heart

star

oval

diamond

# Words for Places

school
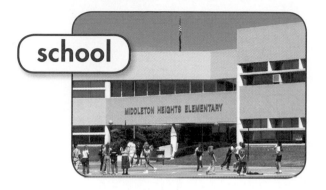

home

park

train station

police station

fire station

post office

library

# Words for Animals

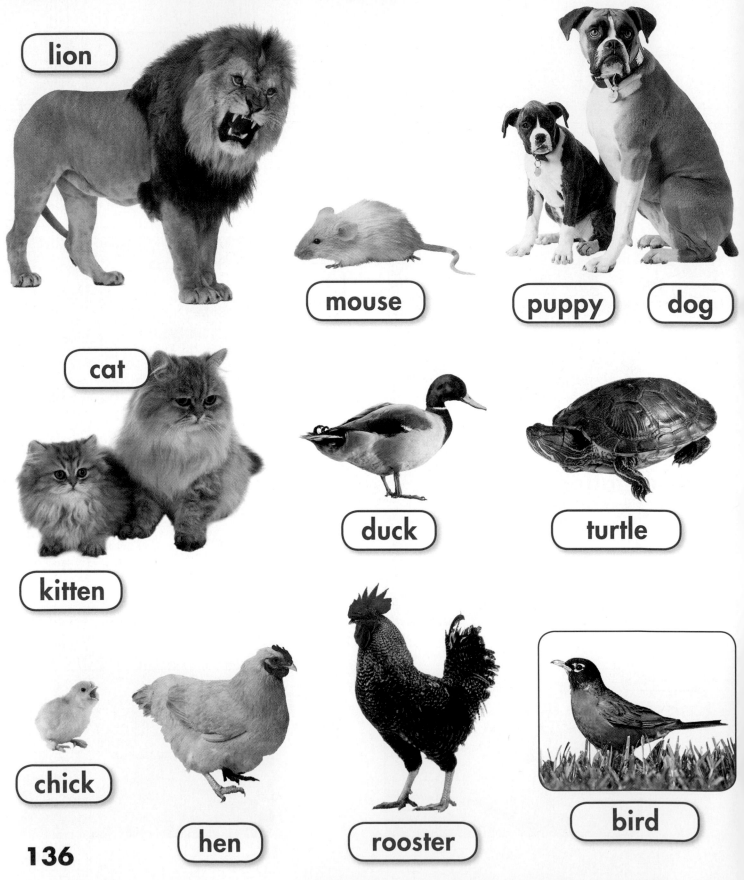

lion

mouse

puppy

dog

cat

duck

turtle

kitten

chick

hen

rooster

bird

136

butterfly

fish

whale

caterpillar

bear

panda

beaver

calf

cow

137

# Words for Actions

skip

walk

run

fly

swim

ride

jump

hop

# Position Words

up

in

out

on

around

down

over

under

# My Classroom

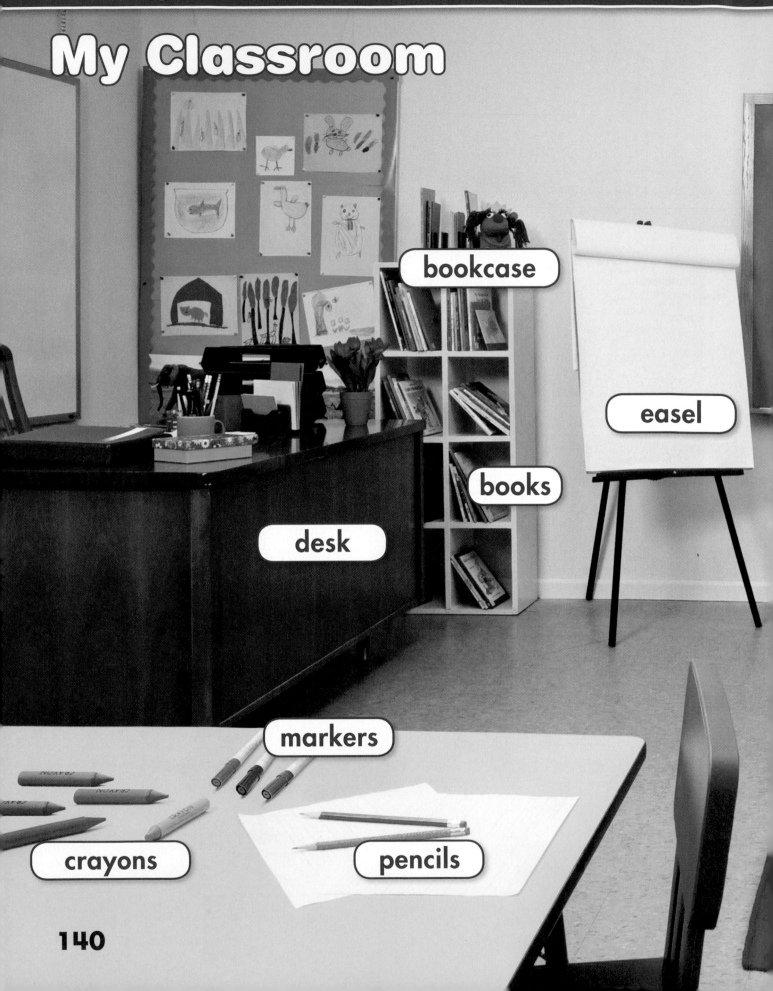

bookcase

easel

books

desk

markers

crayons

pencils

teacher

toys

paper

chair

blocks

table

rug

# Words for Feelings

happy

frightened

worried

excited

angry

proud

sad

surprised

# My Family

mom
mother

dad
father

sister

grandmother

grandfather

brother

# Acknowledgments

## Illustrations

**Cover:** Rob Hefferan

**12** Natalia Vasquez

**28, 32, 48, 69, 88–89, 108–109** Mick Reid

**30–31** Paul Meisel

**50–51** Colleen Madden

**52** Carolyn Croll

**59–65** Maria Mola

**70–71** Carolina Farias

**72** Susan Mitchell

**79–85** Wednesday Kirwan

**90–91** David Austin Clar

**92** Anthony Lewis

**99–105** Cale Atkinson

**110–111** Remy Simard

**112** Jannie Ho

**119–125** Robbie Short.

## Photographs

Every effort has been made to secure permission and provide appropriate credit for photographic material. The publisher deeply regrets any omission and pledges to correct errors called to its attention in subsequent editions.

Unless otherwise acknowledged, all photographs are the property of Pearson Education, Inc.

Photo locators denoted as follows: Top (T), Center (C), Bottom (B), Left (L), Right (R), Background (Bkgd)

**10** (B) ©William Leaman/Alamy

**49** Cyril Laubscher/©DK Images, Dave King/©DK Images, Geoff Brightling/©DK Images, Mike Dunning/©DK Images

**68** ©DK Images, Jane Burton/©DK Images

**130** (T) ©DK Images

**131** (T, B) ©DK Images.